August 19, 2010

The Honorable Darrell Issa
Ranking Member
Committee on Oversight and Government Reform
House of Representatives

Subject: *Carbon Trading: Current Situation and Oversight Considerations for Policymakers*

Dear Mr. Issa:

This letter transmits to you our briefing slides in response to your request concerning carbon trading in the United Sates and various design and implementation issues to be considered in discussions about a possible national carbon trading program. Industrial activities in the United States emit significant amounts of carbon dioxide and other greenhouse gases each year, substantially affecting the earth's climate, according to the National Academy of Sciences. In an effort to reduce these emissions, some have suggested capping emissions and allowing them to be traded in secondary markets just as other commodities are traded. We briefed your committee staff on the results of our work on July 23, 2010. Specifically, we provided information on (1) carbon-related products currently traded in the United States and the extent of trading; (2) risks and challenges posed by these products; (3) the extent to which and how these products are regulated; and (4) issues that market observers identified for policymaker consideration as part of creating a national cap-and-trade carbon market. The attached briefing slides were updated to reflect additional information as discussed during the briefing, including how carbon products are also subject to political and regulatory risk and how they are treated under laws applicable to transactions in commodities.

We reviewed publicly available reports, congressional testimonies, and federal laws; reports from GAO, Congressional Research Service, and the Congressional Budget Office; studies and reports from several professional associations, World Bank, and academics; and information from, among others, the Commodity Futures Trading Commission (CFTC), Chicago Climate Exchange, Chicago Climate Futures Exchange, New York Mercantile Exchange (NYMEX), and European Climate Exchange. We also met with knowledgeable staff at CFTC and the U.K. Financial Services Authority, industry associations, U.S. and European exchanges, a carbon emitter, financial institution, and academics known as experts on carbon trading.

We conducted this performance audit from April 2010 to August 2010, in accordance with generally accepted government auditing standards. Those standards require that we plan and perform the audit to obtain sufficient, appropriate evidence to provide a reasonable basis for our findings and conclusions based on our audit objectives. We believe that the evidence obtained provides a reasonable basis for our findings and conclusions based on our audit objectives.

Summary

Various carbon products are traded in the United States, but volumes have been small compared to other commodity markets. The products traded include carbon allowances, which entitle the holder to emit a specific amount of a greenhouse gas, and carbon offsets, which are measurable reductions of greenhouse gas emissions from an activity or project in one location that are used to compensate for emissions occurring elsewhere.[1] Derivatives on carbon products are also traded in the United States, including primarily futures contracts.[2] Although no official measure of volume of trading exists, various sources estimated that from $2.4 billion to $2.7 billion of carbon products traded in United States in 2009, with offsets accounting for around $74 million.[3] U.S. carbon trading volumes appear to have fallen sharply in 2010, with volumes of RGGI allowances trading at around 15 percent of their 2009 levels as of June 2010.

Carbon product trading poses various risks and challenges that were similar to those found in other commodity markets. For example, carbon products pose market risk, which is the exposure to losses from changes in product prices. Similarly, carbon product markets face the risk of potential manipulation and fraud. Although no fraud involving carbon products has been identified in the United States since 2001, carbon products traded in Europe have been part of several fraudulent activities, including those involving value-added tax violations. Carbon markets could be significantly affected by political or regulatory changes after implementation of any U.S. cap-and-trade program, but market observers noted that this risk could be mitigated by including elements in the program that increased certainty of its duration and features.

Under the Commodity Exchange Act (CEA) carbon emissions are considered to be an "exempt commodity." Before Congress amended the CEA in the recently enacted Dodd-Frank Wall Street Reform and Consumer Protection Act (Dodd-Frank Act, Pub. L. No. 111-203), derivatives on exempt commodities were eligible for limited oversight by the primary U.S. commodities regulator, CFTC. They could be traded between qualified parties on an over-the-counter (OTC) basis generally free from CFTC regulation.[4] CFTC's authority over such trading was limited to instances in which CFTC suspected fraud or manipulation. Although typical transactions in carbon emissions qualified for OTC trading, to date market participants have traded carbon products mostly on exchanges subject to CFTC's full authority. The Dodd-Frank amendments, which are not yet in effect, replaced this regime with clearing requirements and other requirements intended to increase transparency of the OTC derivatives market and reduce the potential for counterparty and systemic risk. The amendments provide an exemption from clearing, exchange trading, and other requirements for counterparties that qualify as end users.

The market participants, academics, regulators, and other market observers that we spoke with identified several issues for policymakers' consideration in the event that the United States implements a national cap-and-trade program. Some noted that the design of the primary carbon market can significantly affect the secondary carbon market. For example,

---

[1] Offsets are typically quantified in metric tons—2,205 pounds—of carbon dioxide equivalent. An example of an offset project is a system at a waste disposal plant that captures the plant's methane—a greenhouse gas.

[2] Futures are agreements to purchase or sell a commodity for delivery in the future. Like other types of derivatives, their prices are based on the value of an underlying commodity.

[3] These estimates included those by the World Bank and Point Carbon, an industry consulting firm.

[4] Exempt commodities include all commodities other than those specifically designated in law as agricultural (such as corn or wheat) or as excluded (such as interest rates or currencies).

the liquidity of trading in the secondary markets could be limited if emissions caps are set too high or if emitters are not allowed to hold or "bank" emissions allowances for future use. Observers also saw value to allowing both exchange-based and OTC carbon trading as a way to increase the ability of participants to manage their specific risks and allow for innovation, although the recent financial crisis highlighted that OTC trading can create credit exposures that can sometimes pose systemic concerns if overly concentrated. Given these risks, effective oversight of secondary market trading under a national cap-and-trade program may depend on the adequacy of CFTC's surveillance authority and its level of resources. The Dodd-Frank Act requires that an interagency working group to be chaired by the CFTC Chairman study the oversight of existing and prospective carbon markets to ensure an efficient, secure, and transparent carbon market.[5]

Conclusions and Recommendation for Executive Action

Although carbon products pose risks similar to those posed by other commodities traded currently, the potential for the existence of fraudulent activities reinforces the importance of ensuring that any trading associated with a national cap-and-trade program is adequately regulated. The study of the interagency working group called for in the Dodd-Frank Act offers an opportunity to further explore and better understand how one would develop an efficient, secure, and transparent carbon trading market. Having this group consider the issues we identified relating to alternative designs of the primary and secondary markets and the regulatory oversight of these markets would be helpful in making any decisions on the design and oversight of existing and prospective carbon markets.

We recommend that the Chairman of the CFTC ensure that the interagency working group created by the Dodd-Frank Act explores (1) how the design of any primary carbon market could affect the liquidity of any secondary market trading; (2) the structure of the secondary market, including the role OTC markets may play in carbon trading; and (3) the resources federal regulators may need to effectively oversee domestic carbon markets.

Agency Comments

We provided CFTC a draft of this report for review and comment. In an e-mail the CFTC's Senior Counsel, Legislative Affairs, stated that the issues we highlighted in our report will be raised and considered during further study of carbon trading. CFTC also provided technical comments, which we incorporated as appropriate.

As arranged with your office, unless you publicly announce the contents of this report earlier, we plan no further distribution until 30 days from the report date. At that time, we will send copies to the Chairman, CFTC, and interested congressional committees. This report will be available at no charge on GAO's Web site at http://www.gao.gov.

---

[5]Pub. L. No. 111-203 § 750 (2010).

If you or your staff have questions regarding this report, please contact me at (202) 512-8678 or williamso@gao.gov. Contact points for our Offices of Congressional Relations and Public Affairs may be found on the last page of this report. Key contributors are listed in enclosure II.

Sincerely yours,

Orice Williams Brown
Director, Financial Markets
  and Community Investment

Enclosures-2

Briefing for Ranking Member, House Committee on Oversight and Government Reform

Carbon Trading:
Current Situation and Oversight
Considerations for Policymakers

Briefing Outline

- Introduction

- Objectives

- Scope and Methodology

- Summary of Findings

- Background

- Findings

- Conclusions and Recommendation for Executive Action

- Attachment I—Additional Details on European Emission Credits, Allowances, and Trading Associated with Them

- Attachment II—States Included in U.S. Regional Cap-and-trade Programs

2

Introduction

- Industrial activities in the United States emit significant amounts of carbon dioxide (CO_2) and other greenhouse gases each year that have substantial effects on the earth's climate, according to the National Academy of Sciences.

- Some have suggested that these emissions could be priced and traded as a commodity as part of a broader effort to efficiently reduce national carbon emissions, known as cap-and-trade.

- A cap-and-trade system for sulfur dioxide (SO_2) began in 1995 and has been in use in Europe since 2005 for greenhouse gases.

- Pending legislation in Congress would establish a cap-and-trade system for greenhouse gas emissions in the United States.

3

Introduction (cont'd)

- Carbon trading is seen as a cost-efficient way to control greenhouse gases, but also raises a number of potential concerns and uncertainty about how to ensure that such trading is effectively overseen and regulated.

- Ranking Member Issa of the House Committee on Oversight and Government Reform asked us to study the viability of a carbon offset market and evaluate whether the government was prepared to manage and oversee it. This briefing examines factors to consider in designing and regulating a national secondary carbon trading market. As part of this request, GAO will report on the design of carbon offsets.

- A *carbon offset* is a measurable reduction of greenhouse gas emissions from an activity or project in one location that is used to compensate for emissions occurring elsewhere.
  - Offsets are typically quantified in metric tons—2,205 pounds—of carbon dioxide equivalent.
  - An example of an offset project is a system at a waste disposal landfill that captures the landfill's methane, which is a greenhouse gas.

- For the purpose of this briefing, the *primary market* is the point at which emission allowances would be distributed and offsets are created. In the *secondary market*, participants purchase the emission allowances and carbon offset credits or conduct transactions involving derivatives relating to carbon products.

4

Objectives

1. What carbon-related products are currently traded in the United States, and what is the extent of trading?

2. What risks and challenges do these products pose?

3. To what extent and how are these products regulated?

4. What issues were identified by market observers for policymaker consideration as part of creating a national carbon market?

5

Scope and Methodology

- We reviewed documentary evidence, including
  - publicly available reports, congressional testimonies, and federal laws;
  - reports from GAO, Congressional Research Service, and the Congressional Budget Office;
  - studies and reports from several professional associations, World Bank, and academics; and
  - information from, among others, Commodity Futures Trading Commission (CFTC), Chicago Climate Exchange, Chicago Climate Futures Exchange, New York Mercantile Exchange (NYMEX), and European Climate Exchange.

- We interviewed market observers, including officials and staff from organizations currently participating in or researching carbon markets, including
  - domestic and international regulators (CFTC and the U.K. Financial Services Authority);
  - industry association groups (International Emissions Trading Association and International Swaps and Derivatives Association);
  - U.S. and European exchanges; and
  - academics known as experts on carbon trading.

- We conducted this performance audit from April 2010 to August 2010, in accordance with generally accepted government auditing standards. Those standards require that we plan and perform the audit to obtain sufficient, appropriate evidence to provide a reasonable basis for our findings and conclusions based on our audit objectives. We believe that the evidence obtained provides a reasonable basis for our findings and conclusions based on our audit objectives.

6

Summary of Findings

- A variety of carbon products currently trade in the United States, but trading volumes are small, and most trades take place on organized exchanges rather than in over-the-counter (OTC) markets.

- Carbon products traded in the U.S. carbon markets have risks similar to those posed by other commodity products and have experienced problems (including fraud) domestically and internationally. The risk that political or regulatory changes could affect the carbon markets was a concern, but market observers noted it could be mitigated in the program's design.

- Most of the carbon trading to date in the United States has occurred on regulated futures markets and is subject to the regulatory jurisdiction of CFTC.

- Market observers in the United States and elsewhere identified several issues for consideration by policymakers relating to the design and regulation of a carbon market if the United States creates a national cap-and-trade program.

7

Background

Under cap-and-trade programs, governments reduce the overall amount of greenhouse gas emissions by granting regulated entities limited allowances to emit and allowing the entities to trade allowances among themselves.

- Each allowance represents a set quantity of greenhouse gas emissions, such as 1 metric ton. Regulated entities must surrender enough allowances for all of their emissions at the end of specified time periods.

- Regulated entities need to hold allowances for their emissions and each allowance would entitle them to emit a specific amount of a greenhouse gas.

- Governments distribute carbon allowances in the primary market by selling them, distributing them for free to regulated entities, or both.

- If a regulated entity's emissions exceeds the number of carbon allowances it receives or purchases in the primary market, it can purchase additional allowances in the secondary market or, if the cap-and-trade program allows it, purchase carbon offset credits.

- Carbon offset credits can be serialized and accounted for in a registry or other approved tracking system to help ensure that they are traded and transferred legitimately. For example, a centralized registry can be used to help prevent double counting of offset credits.

Background (cont'd)

The European Union has a cap-and-trade program for certain sectors, but currently the United States has only a regional cap-and-trade program that limits emissions from certain power plants in participating states

- The European Union created its Emission Trading Scheme (ETS) to help EU member states meet their Kyoto Protocol commitments. The protocol set binding emissions targets for 37 industrialized countries and the European Community to achieve between 2008 and 2012.

  - Under the Kyoto Protocol's Clean Development Mechanism, countries with binding emission targets can implement projects that reduce or avoid emissions—such as the construction of infrastructure for renewable energy (e.g., wind, solar, renewable fuels) projects—in a developing country that does not have a binding emissions target under the protocol. These projects earn Certified Emissions Reduction credits (carbon offsets) that an industrialized country sponsoring the project can sell or use to comply with its Kyoto target. These credits, along with carbon allowances and derivatives on those allowances, are traded on several markets. (See attachment I for more detail.)

- The industrialized countries' Kyoto Protocol emissions targets are tracked in national registry systems. As of May 2010, there were 37 national registries, an European Community registry, and a Clean Development Mechanism registry, which is used to issue and distribute the offset credits generated under that mechanism to the national registries.

  - The ETS currently covers emissions from power plants; certain industrial sectors, such as oil refining, cement, and glass; and aviation.

9

GAO-10-851R Carbon Trading

Background (cont'd)

- Currently, the United States has one regional cap-and-trade program in operation, but other regional cap-and-trade programs are in various stages of development.

- The Regional Greenhouse Gas Initiative (RGGI) was created in 2005 and regulates the carbon dioxide emissions of large fossil fuel electricity generators in 10 participating northeastern and mid-Atlantic states.

- Other states are currently developing regional greenhouse gas initiatives. The Midwestern Greenhouse Gas Reduction Accord is an agreement among six midwestern states and one Canadian province to establish a greenhouse gas reduction program. The Western Climate Initiative is a collaboration among seven states and four Canadian provinces that aims to tackle climate change through a regional cap-and-trade program and other initiatives. (See attachment II for the members of each regional program).

10

Background (cont'd)

- Regulators told us that emission reduction programs depend on the timely registration of carbon allowances and offsets in registries. Existing registries include, among others:

  - The Climate Registry, a nonprofit collaboration among North American states, provinces, territories, and Native Sovereign Nations that sets standards to calculate, verify, and publicly report greenhouse gas emissions.

  - The California Climate Action Registry, a program of the Climate Action Reserve that serves as a voluntary greenhouse gas registry to protect and promote early actions to reduce greenhouse gas emissions by organizations.

11

1. Current Carbon Trading

In the absence of a national cap-and-trade program, the volume of carbon trading in the United States has been modest.

- No centralized official measure of market volumes exists, but the World Bank and Point Carbon, an industry tracking firm, estimated the value of the total U.S. carbon market at around $2.4 billion to $2.7 billion in 2009.

  - In the allowance market, the World Bank estimates that in the ETS, $119 billion worth of allowances and derivatives changed hands in 2009, compared to about $2.2 billion in the United States ($50 million on the Chicago Climate Exchange and $2.18 billion in RGGI). In a recent report, Point Carbon found that the volume of RGGI allowances traded in the first half of 2010 was less than 15 percent of RGGI allowances traded in all of 2009.

  - In the offset market, Point Carbon estimates that in 2009, offsets purchased by organizations located in the United States represented 0.2 percent of the global carbon offset market, or approximately $74 million.

1. Current Carbon Trading (cont'd)

- Of the trading that occurs in the U.S. carbon market, offsets, which tend to be unique transactions, are generally traded on OTC markets, while allowances, which are more standardized products, are generally traded on exchanges.

- Bilateral OTC markets allow eligible parties to enter into bilateral contracts directly, without using an exchange. In the carbon market, OTC contracts are made predominantly between emitters and liquidity providers, such as financial intermediaries.

- In 2009, the value of the OTC/bilateral offset market was approximately $64 million of the $74 million market total, according to Point Carbon, with exchange trading accounting for the remaining $10 million.

13

1. Current Carbon Trading (cont'd)

Various types of allowances, offsets, and other carbon products are or expected to be traded in the United States.

- Allowances are traded as part of various mandatory and voluntary programs.

  - For example, electric power generators covered by RGGI and others can buy, sell, and trade emissions allowances.

  - In a voluntary market active in the United States, participants on the Chicago Climate Exchange agree to limit their emissions to certain levels. They are then issued certain numbers of standardized carbon financial instruments, each representing 100 metric tons of CO_2 equivalent that exchange participants can trade among themselves.

1. Current Carbon Trading (cont'd)

- Offsets are also traded as part of these programs in the United States.

  - By registering an offset project with the Chicago Climate Exchange, members can receive Carbon Financial Instruments they can trade on that exchange.

  - The Climate Action Reserve in California is a voluntary offsets program that issues carbon offset credits known as "climate reserve tonnes," which can be registered and traded among the reserve's participants nationwide.

  - RGGI allows offsets that can be used for compliance, but to date allowances have been sufficient to meet current demand, and no offsets have been issued.

15

1. Current Carbon Trading (cont'd)

- Derivatives are traded on underlying allowances and offsets.

  - To facilitate efficient trading and risk management, derivatives, including futures contracts and other products, are traded on U.S. carbon products.

    - Futures are agreements to purchase or sell a commodity for delivery in the future. Like other types of derivatives, their prices are based on the value of an underlying commodity.

    - For example, a subsidiary of Chicago Climate Exchange—the Chicago Climate Futures Exchange—trades futures that call for the future delivery of Chicago Climate Exchange's carbon financial instruments. This exchange also trades futures on RGGI allowances and Climate Action Reserve's climate reserve tonnes offsets. Another exchange, NYMEX's Green Exchange Venture (Green Exchange), also trades futures on RGGI allowances and climate reserve tonnes.

    - The Chicago Climate Futures Exchange and the Green Exchange also trade futures on Certified Emission Reduction credits, and the Green Exchange trades futures on EU allowances.

1. Current Carbon Trading (cont'd)

- Options contracts are traded on U.S. carbon exchanges.

  - Options allow a purchaser the right, but not the obligation, to buy or sell a specified amount of the underlying asset for a specified price within a specified time in the future.

  - The Chicago Climate Futures Exchange trades options and futures. The Green Exchange also trades options on the same products it uses for futures contracts.

- Derivatives, including forward contracts and options, are also traded in OTC markets.

  - Forwards are non-standardized contracts that obligate the seller to deliver assets to the buyer at a pre-determined time in the future at an agreed-upon price.

  - Options can also be customized and traded off exchange in OTC markets.

  - None of the sources we reviewed provided a clear estimate of the extent to which forward contracts and options on carbon products are traded OTC.

1. Current Carbon Trading (cont'd)

Adopting a mandatory cap-and-trade program in the United States could create the largest carbon market in the world.

- According to two industry observers, the sheer size of the U.S. economy means that if the United States established a mandatory cap-and-trade program, the resulting market for carbon emissions products would become the largest in the world, attracting traders from around the globe.

2. Risks and Challenges

Trading carbon offset credits and other products poses market, credit, and operational risks similar to those in other commodity markets, although political risk can also be a concern.

- Market risk arises from changes in asset prices.

  - Prices of carbon products fluctuate because of changes in supply and demand, economic conditions, and costs of carbon abatement.

- Some academics noted that carbon markets could have significant price volatility.

  - According to one economist, carbon prices are prone to extreme volatility because the supply of allowances is relatively fixed and the demand for allowances changes little in the short run.
  - Large price swings can result from unanticipated changes in economic activity, weather, fuel prices, or technological developments.

2. Risks and Challenges (cont'd)

- Carbon products also can present credit and operational risks.

  - Credit risk is the potential for a seller to fail to meet its obligations in accordance with agreed terms.

  - Carbon products could produce operational risk losses if a holder does not have adequate internal risk management or other systems in place.

20

2. Risks and Challenges (cont'd)

- Trading in carbon products could also be affected by the risk of political or regulatory uncertainty.

  - Trading volumes, prices, and the number of participants willing to trade could fall if certain legislative, regulatory, or legal actions significantly changed the design and implementation of a U.S. cap-and-trade program.

  - Market participants said that political and regulatory uncertainty would have to be mitigated by designing a U.S. cap-and-trade program that has a long time frame, no early sunset provisions, and other elements that increase the certainty of the program's structure or that reduce the potential for significant changes after implementation.

2. Risks and Challenges (cont'd)

Like other financial products, market manipulation would be a risk in carbon markets.

- As with any commodity product, allowances could be subject to attempts to amass positions with the intent of manipulating prices. Participants may attempt to artificially reduce supply, particularly if not enough allowances are available for trading.

- For example, a trader might attempt to "corner" the market by amassing a large inventory of allowances while simultaneously taking futures or forward positions that required others to make delivery to it. As a result, other traders with delivery obligations that they must fulfill are "squeezed" into buying from the manipulator at inflated prices.

- CFTC staff and academics we interviewed told us that while the risk of market manipulation exists, it would not be unique to carbon trading and also exists in the trading of other commodity products.

- According to one economist, the risk of cornering the carbon allowance market would likely be low, provided a large volume of allowances is available and demand for them is widespread, making it difficult for any one participant to accumulate enough to manipulate prices.

2. Risks and Challenges (cont'd)

As with other commodities, carbon trading is not immune to fraudulent activities.

- Market observers we interviewed told us that recent types of fraud are not unique to carbon but can happen in any newly traded product market.

  - Although regulators have not identified any recent fraud in the United States, from 1999 through 2001, an emissions trader ran a Ponzi scheme involving California's pollution trading program. Such schemes involve paying purported returns to existing investors from funds contributed by new investors. According to one market observer, these schemes may be more likely to occur in newly created markets, because potential investors do not fully understand how the markets operate.

  - Some market observers told us that carbon products were recently subject to carousel fraud relating to the value added tax systems used in various European countries. In these cases, parties bought carbon allowances in one country without paying tax and sold them in another country, pocketing the tax included in the price of the allowance.

2. Risks and Challenges (cont'd)

- In 2010, another fraud in Germany involved use of a "phishing" scheme (using false e-mail and a fake Web site) to obtain carbon trading account information for individual accounts on national carbon registries that were part of the ETS. The rogue traders were able to carry out a number of transactions before they were discovered.

- Other fraud cases involving carbon products can also occur under cap-and-trade programs, such as reselling offset credits that have already been surrendered for compliance or that do not represent verified emissions reductions. As noted above, no such cases have been identified in the United States.

- Several national audit offices told us that they were planning to conduct reviews of carbon trading activities soon.

3. Current Regulation

Carbon emissions are considered to be an "exempt commodity" under the Commodity Exchange Act and the primary U.S. commodities products regulator—CFTC—will have limited authority to act over any OTC trading until a more extensive regulatory regime takes effect for OTC transactions under the Dodd-Frank Act.

- Exempt commodities include all commodities other than those specifically designated in law as agricultural (such as corn or wheat) or as excluded (such as interest rates or currencies).

- For exempt commodities trading on an OTC basis, CFTC can only act if it suspects fraud or manipulation is occurring.

3. Current Regulation (cont'd)

However, the majority of trading in carbon products in the United States to date has been of products traded on a fully-regulated futures exchange over which CFTC has full authority.

- As noted earlier, most of the carbon trading in the United States has occurred through the RGGI futures contract traded on the Chicago Climate Futures Exchange.

- Because this market is registered with CFTC as a designated contract market, it is subject to the full range of CFTC oversight.

- For trading on designated contract markets, CFTC can take various steps to detect fraudulent or abusive trading practices, including daily monitoring of electronic trading. It can also perform examinations of these exchanges and their members' activities and require participants to provide reports of activities to CFTC.

3. Current Regulation (cont'd)

- Carbon products traded on an OTC basis are subject to more limited or no CFTC oversight, depending on how trades occur.

- Trades on the Chicago Climate Exchange are considered part of the OTC market and are subject to more limited CFTC oversight.

  - The Chicago Climate Exchange is registered as an exempt commercial market (ECM), which is an OTC electronic trading facility for commodities that are not specifically named in law as agricultural or as excluded commodities. Trades on this market are allowed between eligible commercial entities, which are large, sophisticated participants that trade on a principal-to-principal basis.

  - CFTC's authority over trading on an exempt commercial market like the Chicago Climate Exchange is more limited than its authority over designated contract markets. Transactions on an exempt commercial market generally are not subject to substantive regulation by CFTC or its enforcement jurisdiction, except for its fraud and manipulation authority. However, if CFTC determines that a contract has a significant price discovery function (i.e., is used by other market participants to determine the price for a commodity) it can subject the ECM to extensive CFTC oversight and responsibilities with respect to that contract.

  - CFTC cannot routinely examine or require periodic reporting from ECMs or their participants that are trading products not determined to perform a significant price discovery function.

  - CFTC can request information on trading on ECMs if it receives allegations of fraud or suspects manipulation.

3. Current Regulation (cont'd)

- CFTC does not oversee other OTC trading and does not oversee distribution of allowances and offsets in the primary markets, although it could seek information and take action in the event of perceived attempts to manipulate the prices of the carbon futures on the two U.S. designated contract markets over which it has authority.

3. Current Regulation (cont'd)

Other authorities could act in the event of problems relating to carbon products.

- Unlawful activities associated with carbon products could be subject to actions by the Federal Trade Commission (FTC) and/or criminal/civil law enforcement agencies such as the Department of Justice (DOJ) and state authorities. For example, a fraudulent scheme involving carbon offsets might constitute an anticompetitive or unfair trade practice subject to FTC jurisdiction or anticompetitive or criminal conduct subject to the jurisdiction of DOJ and state authorities.

- As a result of the Dodd-Frank Wall Street Reform and Consumer Protection Act (Pub. L. No. 111-203, title VII), CFTC will provide greater oversight of many OTC derivative products, including carbon products. The Dodd-Frank Act that was recently signed into law includes various provisions that would change requirements applicable to OTC derivatives and generally would require standardized contracts to be cleared on central clearinghouses.[1]

---

[1]Pub. L. No: 111-203, 2010.

4. Design and Regulatory Issues for Any National Cap-and-Trade Carbon Market

Market observers we spoke with noted several issues associated with the design of the primary carbon market that could affect the success of secondary trading of carbon products in the financial markets.

- The level at which emissions caps are set in primary markets can affect secondary markets' liquidity (the ability to buy or sell without causing large price movements). For example, in Phase I of the ETS, market observers said that the cap was set too high, and trading and prices declined significantly with the onset of the current recession.

- Allowing participants to hold or "bank" allowances or having the allowances expire after a certain time period could also affect secondary market trading. Allowing the banking of allowances can, among other things, allow for longer-term financial products.

- Ensuring that adequate and timely requirements are in place to register allowances also could help maintain the integrity of the secondary market for carbon products. CFTC staff, several economists, and exchange officials noted that providing timely information to recognized carbon registries would be necessary to ensure that allowances and offsets were not used more than once. For example, the Hungarian government resold surrendered credits. These duplicative transactions have been unwound, and regulation has been enhanced to prevent this type of error from occurring again.

4. Design and Regulatory Issues for Any National Cap-and-Trade Carbon Market (cont'd)

Market participants and observers supported allowing carbon products to be traded in OTC markets as well as exchanges.

- Various market observers we spoke with supported allowing wide participation in the markets as a way of increasing liquidity and saw allowing carbon products to be traded on OTC markets as well as on exchanges as a way of increasing participation.

  - OTC markets may allow for emitters to become innovative at managing their risks. According to market observers and participants, when the EU markets were being developed, the OTC markets helped facilitate innovation and risk management.

  - OTC markets allow for customized contracts, variable collateral requirements, and the ability to negotiate prices bilaterally.
    - Market observers noted that having OTC markets would allow counterparties the flexibility to structure nonstandardized contracts. For example, most exchange-traded futures contracts trade only a limited number of years into the future (typically 3-5 years), but in some cases, contracts may need to be extended several years or decades.
    - OTC markets could attract a wide range of participants, increasing the capital available to the carbon markets.

- Although offering benefits, OTC activities can also pose risks, including systemic risk, counterparty credit risk, and concentration risk. Our recent work involving credit default swaps illustrated that OTC markets can lack transparency that creates uncertainty over the levels of risks in such markets and the extent to which risk exposures are concentrated.[2]

[2]GAO, *Systemic Risk: Regulatory Oversight and Recent Initiatives to Address Risks Posed by Credit Default Swaps, GAO-09-397T* (Washington, D.C.: Mar. 5, 2009).

4. Design and Regulatory issues for Any National Cap-and-Trade Carbon Market (cont'd)

Additional mechanisms to better ensure effective oversight and interagency coordination could be important to the success of U.S. carbon markets.

- Because CFTC does not have clear authority to act over all trading activities, carbon markets might not be effectively overseen and regulated. Our work examining issues related to credit default swaps indicated that having multiple regulators that individually lacked complete authority hampered U.S. regulators' efforts to monitor and manage the potential systemic risk arising from those products.

- Sufficient CFTC resources would be needed to ensure effective oversight of a carbon market. CFTC officials told us that while their agency would be able to leverage its existing surveillance system, it would need more people and more resources to oversee the volume of trading likely to develop under a national cap-and-trade program.

32

4. Design and Regulatory Issues for Any National Cap-and-Trade Carbon Market (cont'd)

- In addition to CFTC, other agencies are likely to have important roles in a national cap-and-trade program, such as the Environmental Protection Agency, which might administer the primary market, and the U.S. Department of Agriculture, which could be involved in administering certain agricultural offsets.

- U.S. regulators that must cooperate with other domestic or international bodies often use formal memorandums of understanding to specify how such interactions occur.

  - CFTC has such memorandums with such entities as the Securities and Exchange Commission and with foreign commodities regulators.

- Although CFTC staff told us that they are already coordinating with the U.S. Department of Agriculture and the Environmental Protection Agency, it has yet to establish such memorandums with these agencies.

4. Design and Regulatory issues for Any National Cap-and-Trade Carbon Market (cont'd)

- Section 750 of the Dodd-Frank Act requires that an interagency working group conduct a study on the oversight of existing and prospective carbon markets to ensure an efficient, secure, and transparent carbon market, including oversight of spot markets and derivative markets.

- This interagency group is to be chaired by the Chairman of CFTC and includes the Secretary of Agriculture, the Secretary of the Treasury, the Chairman of the Securities and Exchange Commission, the Administrator of the Environmental Protection Agency, the Chairman of the Federal Energy Regulatory Commission, the Commissioner of the Federal Trade Commission, and the Administrator of the Energy Information Administration.

Conclusions and Recommendation for Executive Action

Conclusions.

- Trading of carbon products has been limited to date in the United States. Our work identified various issues that require further exploration as part of the debate surrounding the creation of a national mandatory cap-and-trade program.

- Although carbon products pose risks similar to those posed by other commodities that are traded currently, the potential for fraudulent activities reinforces the importance of ensuring that any trading associated with a national cap-and-trade program is adequately regulated.

- The study of the interagency working group called for in the Dodd-Frank Act offers an opportunity to further explore and better understand how to develop an efficient, secure, and transparent carbon trading market. Although its mandated areas for study were broad, having this group consider the issues identified in this briefing relating to alternative designs for the primary and secondary markets and the regulatory oversight of these markets would be helpful in making any decisions on the design and oversight of existing and prospective carbon markets.

Conclusions and Recommendation for Executive Action (cont'd)

Recommendation for Executive Action.

In his capacity as chair of the working group addressing the design and regulation of carbon markets under a national cap-and-trade program, we recommend that the CFTC Chairman explore (1) how the design of any primary carbon market could affect the liquidity of any secondary market trading; (2) the structure of the secondary market, including the role OTC markets may play in carbon trading; and (3) the resources federal regulators may need to effectively oversee domestic carbon markets.

Attachment I: Additional Details on European Emission Allowances, Kyoto Protocol Clean Development Mechanism Offset Credits, and Trading Associated with Them

- Certified Emission Reduction credits (CER) generated by Clean Development Mechanism projects can be used by industrialized countries to meet their Kyoto targets. Regulated entities can also use a limited amount of CERs to satisfy their compliance obligations under the EU Emission Trading Scheme (ETS).

  - Each CER is equivalent to 1 metric ton of carbon dioxide.

  - CERs are issued for projects that meet several key requirements, including review by national officials of the country where the project occurs and independent validation of the emission reduction.

- Countries participating in the ETS issue EU allowances (EUA).

  - EUAs are tradable emissions allowances that regulated entities can surrender to cover emission of 1 ton of carbon dioxide equivalent.

  - The amount of EUAs allocated to regulated entity is set out in national allocation plans prepared by the member states.

Attachment I: Additional Details on European Emission Allowances, Kyoto Protocol Clean Development Mechanism Offset Credits, and Trading Associated with Them (cont'd)

- Kyoto Protocol emission targets for industrialized countries are expressed as levels of allowed emissions, or assigned amounts units (AAU). Under the protocol's emission trading mechanism, AAUs can be traded. Each AAU equates to one ton of CO_2 equivalent. Because the United States is not a party to the protocol, it does not have AAUs and is not eligible to trade them.

- IntercontinentalExchange (ICE) Futures Europe is the world's largest carbon market and trades instruments very similar to those already used in the United States.

- According to an exchange official, at least 90 percent of the world carbon products are European Climate Exchange contracts traded on ICE. These markets offer several products, including

  - Original instruments—CERs and EUAs;

  - Futures and options on CERs and EUAs; and

  - CER and EUA daily futures contracts, which are like contracts for the buying and selling of physical products.

Attachment II: States Included in U.S. Regional Cap-and-trade Programs

- RGGI includes 10 states—Connecticut, Delaware, Maine, Maryland, Massachusetts, New Hampshire, New Jersey, New York, Rhode Island, and Vermont—as members; Pennsylvania and 3 Canadian provinces—New Brunswick, Ontario, and Quebec—are observers.

- Midwestern Greenhouse Gas Reduction Accord includes 6 states—Iowa, Illinois, Kansas, Michigan, Minnesota, Wisconsin—and 1 Canadian province—Manitoba—as members; Indiana, Ohio, and South Dakota and the province of Ontario are observers.

- Western Climate Initiative includes 7 states—Arizona, California, Montana, New Mexico, Oregon, Utah, and Washington—and 4 Canadian provinces—British Columbia, Manitoba, Ontario, and Quebec. Arizona and Utah have dropped out of the cap-and-trade portion of the initiative; Utah may join the cap-and-trade program at a later date; Montana has not yet enacted legislation authorizing the cap-and-trade program; Oregon's participation may depend on the outcome of the gubernatorial election in November 2010; and a California ballot initiative, if approved, would suspend implementation of the state law authorizing the cap-and-trade program until the unemployment rate in California is 5.5 percent or less for a specified time period.

Enclosure II: GAO Contact and Staff Acknowledgments

GAO Contact: Orice Williams Brown (202) 512-8678 or williamso@gao.gov

Staff Acknowledgments: In addition to the individual named above, Cody Goebel, Assistant Director; John Forrester; Mike Hix; Richard Johnson; Jessica Lemke; Akiko Ohnuma; David Rodriguez; Andrew Stavisky; Jeeanette M. Soares; and Paul Thompson made key contributions to this report.

(250538)

GAO's Mission	The Government Accountability Office, the audit, evaluation, and investigative arm of Congress, exists to support Congress in meeting its constitutional responsibilities and to help improve the performance and accountability of the federal government for the American people. GAO examines the use of public funds; evaluates federal programs and policies; and provides analyses, recommendations, and other assistance to help Congress make informed oversight, policy, and funding decisions. GAO's commitment to good government is reflected in its core values of accountability, integrity, and reliability.
Obtaining Copies of GAO Reports and Testimony	The fastest and easiest way to obtain copies of GAO documents at no cost is through GAO's Web site (www.gao.gov). Each weekday afternoon, GAO posts on its Web site newly released reports, testimony, and correspondence. To have GAO e-mail you a list of newly posted products, go to www.gao.gov and select "E-mail Updates."
Order by Phone	The price of each GAO publication reflects GAO's actual cost of production and distribution and depends on the number of pages in the publication and whether the publication is printed in color or black and white. Pricing and ordering information is posted on GAO's Web site, http://www.gao.gov/ordering.htm.
	Place orders by calling (202) 512-6000, toll free (866) 801-7077, or TDD (202) 512-2537.
	Orders may be paid for using American Express, Discover Card, MasterCard, Visa, check, or money order. Call for additional information.
To Report Fraud, Waste, and Abuse in Federal Programs	Contact:
	Web site: www.gao.gov/fraudnet/fraudnet.htm
	E-mail: fraudnet@gao.gov
	Automated answering system: (800) 424-5454 or (202) 512-7470
Congressional Relations	Ralph Dawn, Managing Director, dawnr@gao.gov, (202) 512-4400 U.S. Government Accountability Office, 441 G Street NW, Room 7125 Washington, DC 20548
Public Affairs	Chuck Young, Managing Director, youngc1@gao.gov, (202) 512-4800 U.S. Government Accountability Office, 441 G Street NW, Room 7149 Washington, DC 20548